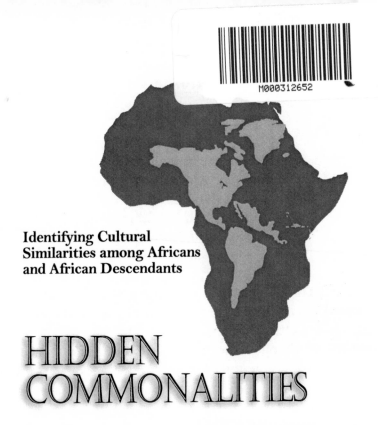

**Identifying Cultural
Similarities among Africans
and African Descendants**

HIDDEN
COMMONALITIES

SAYE CARRIE

LAEL PUBLISHING

HIDDEN COMMONALITIES:
Identifying Cultural Similarities among
Africans and African Descendants
by Saye Carrie
Published by Lael Publishing, LLC
Winston Salem, North Carolina
www.LaelAgency.com

ISBN 978-0-9916515-7-3

For more information:

First Edition

Printed in the United States of America.

"Never suppress who you are because we were all created in a distinctive way."

~Saye Carrie~

TABLE OF CONTENTS

PROLOGUE

"I am not African because I was born in Africa but because Africa was born in me."
~Kwame N'Krumah~

B efore I begin, I would like to give a brief history of my cultural background and describe what inspired me to create this book. I was born in Far Rockaway, Queens, NY of Liberian parentage. Liberia is located off the coast of West Africa, with an area of 43,000 square miles and a population of 4,195,666 people (The World Factbook: Liberia). Liberia is Africa's first independent country; it gained its independence on July 26, 1847(Kraaij, van der, Fred). Liberia is also the second black independent nation, trailing Haiti, which gained its independence on January 1, 1804 (Ott, Thomas O.).

Before the founding of Liberia in 1822, 16 indigenous tribes lived in what was called the 'Pepper Coast', 'Grain Coast, 'Malaguetta Coast, or Costa da Pimenta (these names were given by the European explorers such as the English and Portuguese) The tribes are Mel (consisting of the Gola and Kissi tribes) Kwa (Bassa, Belle, Dei, Grebo, Krahn, Kru), Mande (Bandi, Gio, Kpelle, Lorma, Mandingo, Mano, Mende, Vai). In the course of the 19th century, groups of freed Blacks and Multi-racials from the Southern United States of America repatriated to the west coast of Africa. The colonists called themselves "Americo-

Liberians". The next group are the "Congo" people who are the descendants of freed Black repatriates from the Caribbean, primarily the Barbados. "Congo" people are also recaptured Africans who intercepted from slave vessels by the U.S. Navy after abolishing the slave trade (1806). Many originated from Central Africa, particularly the Congo River Basin (Kraaij, van der, Fred). There are also nomadic tribes like the Fulani, who engage mostly in trade, and the Fanti, who are often fishermen or traders of fish, usually from Ghana, living seasonally and more often permanently in Liberia (Embassy of Liberia 2011-2016). Liberia has people of European descent, many having settled down as miners, missionaries, business people, and so on. Last, there is also a sizeable number of Lebanese, Indians, and other people with Asian roots (Embassy of Liberia 2011-2016). Liberia also consists of a high percentage of a Liberian and Lebanese mixed population. There is also a small minority of Liberians mixed with European, and reside in the country.

I am a descendant of the Kwa (Krahn and Bassa) and Mande-Fu (Lorma), indigenous ethnic group, the repatriated Congo group of the Caribbean (Barbados) and the Congo River Basin, and the Americo-Liberians from the United States.

While spending my entire life in the United Sates, I observed many cultural groups within the Black race. The groups consist of the descendants of enslaved Africans brought to the Americas; such as North America, Latin America, and the Caribbean. There are also Africans who have immigrated to the western hemisphere due to civil wars, Coup d'état, or for better opportunities. Throughout my life, I felt connected to Africans, African-Americans (Black Americans), Afro-Caribbeans (West Indians), as well as Afro-Latinos(nas) (Hispanics). This is so because I was conscious enough to see our hidden similarities, which include food, music, dance, certain customs, hair, language and the struggles we have endured. These groups often clash due to stereotypes, some cultural differences, language, and environmental factors. However yet we share an affinity, which is "Mama Africa". My focus is to dig deep down into our roots and show our commonalities, which can bring unification between us all.

Chapter 1

THE PAN-AFRICAN IDEOLOGY

I have been studying the Pan African ideology for a while because I believe in uplifting the continent of Africa and the African diaspora. Although there are many ethnic groups, regions, and cultures throughout the African continent, we should not let these differences divide us as a people; however, bring us closer. Even though, a lot of our brothers and sisters were stolen and brought to the "New World" they are our family. I am certain those who remained behind mourned for their relatives or friends brought into slavery. Interestingly, we barely hear about this. The diaspora community has European, Asian, and Indigenous American influences; however, we cannot deny the conspicuous impact Africa has made throughout the Black/African diaspora communities worldwide. Even in the continent of Africa, it has faced European colonialism and imperialism. The colonized emulate the colonizer's beliefs and customs because it is viewed as "refined" and "sophisticated "and no longer embrace their traditional culture because it is perceived as "savage like," "evil," or "primitive." It is unfortunate that colonialism and slavery have made most of us divided and not aware of the similarities and destiny we all share.

Pan-Africanism

Pan-Africanism is the idea that people of African descent have the same interests and should be unified. Historically, Pan-Africanism has often taken the shape of the political or cultural movement. In fact, Pan-Africanism is the sentiment that people of African descent have a great deal in common, in which deserves notice and even celebration (Pan Africanism 2016). The Pan African Ideology arose in the late 19th century in counter to European Colonization and exploitation of the African continent. Pan Africanist perspectives held that slavery and colonialism pushed for a negative categorization of race, culture, and values of African people (Adejumobi, Saheed). These detrimental beliefs created intense forms of racism, in which Pan-Africanism sought to eliminate it. Pan-Africanism also focuses on the experiences of African descendants in the Americas. The interest in Africa became significant for some blacks in the "new world" for two prominent reasons. First, due to racial inequality in the USA; which lead African-Americans to plea for voluntary repatriation to Africa. Also, the term "Africans" which had been used by racists as a derogatory description, became a source of identity and pride for Black nationalists (Adejumobi,

Saheed). Due to the awareness of their African identity, black activists in America and throughout the world reclaimed their rights that were denied by western societies.

HIDDEN COMMONALITIES

Chapter 2

PAN-AFRICAN INTELLECTUALS

A few of the early Pan Africanists were Edward Blyden, Henry Sylvester-Williams, W.E.B Dubois and Marcus Garvey.

Edward W. Blyden from St. Thomas is widely known as the father of Pan-Africanism. A way he contributed in this movement was by repatriating to Africa. Specifically, Blyden settled in Liberia, West Africa to teach. Soon after his arrival in 1851, Blyden became employed at Alexander High School in Liberia's capital city Monrovia (Hollis, Lynch Edward). He then started his self-directed studies of theology, the classics, geography, and mathematics. In 1858, Blyden was ordained a Presbyterian Minister and appointed principal of Alexander High school. Blyden was also appointed the editor of the Liberian Herald. The Liberian Herald was the only newspaper in the nation, during President Joseph Jenkins Roberts's presidency. Throughout Blyden's ministry, he would both study scriptures and science to challenge the arguments about Black inferiority that was increasingly popular in Europe and North America. Between 1856 -1877, Blyden authored four books: *A Voice from Bleeding Africa* (1886), *A Vindication of the African Race*; being a Brief Examination of the Arguments in favor of African inferiority 1862; *Africa for Africans* (1872) and *Christianity, Islam and the Negro Race* (1887) and many other works to advance his case. Blyden also opposed the Black and Bi-racial "America-Liberian" elites in Liberia who hoped to monopolize political power. During the 1860s and early 1870s, Blyden was Liberia's secretary of state and professor of classics at Liberia College (Hollis Lynch, Edward). As a secretary of state, he called for the repatriation of skilled and intelligent Afro-West Indians and African-Americans to Liberia.

On the other hand, his proposals drew opposition from the Liberian elite. In 1885, Blyden ran for president of Liberia. After his defeat, he went into self-imposed exile in neighboring Sierra Leone. Edward Wilmont Blyden died in Sierra Leone on February 7, 1912 (Hollis, Lynch Edward).

Another Pan-African intellectual was Henry Sylvester-Williams; a West Indian Barrister formed the African Association in London, England to encourage Pan-African unity, particularly throughout the British colonies. He also connected with African dignitaries. Sylvester-Williams believed that Africans and those of African descent living in the diaspora needed a forum to address their common problems. In 1900, Sylvester-Williams arranged the first Pan

African meeting in collaboration with several black leaders representing various countries of the African diaspora. The meeting consisted of opponents of colonialism and racism. Also, the conference held in London, attracted global attention, placing the word "Pan African" in the lexicon of international affairs and making it part of the standard vocabulary of black intellectuals. The conference also focused on social, political, and economic conditions of blacks in the diaspora, the importance of independent nations governed by people of African descent such as Ethiopia, Haiti, and Liberia, the legacy of slavery and European imperialism, the role of Africa in world history, and the impact of Christianity on the African continent. The final purpose of the conference was for the United States and the imperial European nations to "acknowledge and protect the rights of people of African descent" and to respect the integrity and independence of "the free Black nations of Ethiopia, Haiti, and Liberia (Adejumobi, Saheed A.)."

An influential thinker named William Edward Burghardt (WEB) Dubois was also a Pan African pioneer. Dubois was a consistent advocate for the study of African history and culture. In the turn of the twentieth century, Dubois stated, "the problem of the twentieth century is the problem of the color line." This was not only confined to the issues with Blacks in the United States; however, the statement also addressed the problems that Black Africans living in the continent faced under the European colonial rule (Pan Africanism 2016).

In 1900, Dubois attended the first Pan-African conference held in London, was elected a vice president and wrote the "Address to the Nations of the World" The Niagara movement in a Pan African Department (NAACP History: WEB Du Bois). In 1911, he attended the First Universal Races Congress in London with Black intellectuals from Africa and the West Indies. Du Bois arranged Pan-African congresses around the world in 1919, 1921, 1923, and 1927. The delegations composed of scholars from Africa, the West Indies, and the United States. After the conference, resolutions were created and passed to eradicate colonialism and oppression of Africans. However, little action was taken. During the fifth congress (1945, Manchester, England) elected Du Bois as chairman; however, the power was in the hands of younger Pan Africanist, such as George Padmore and Kwame Nkrumah, who later became significant in the independence movement of their respective countries. Du Bois' final contribution to the Pan-African movement was to take up citizenship in Ghana in 1961 at the request of President Kwame Nkrumah and to begin work as director of the Encyclopedia Africana (NAACP History: WEB Du Bois).

When we further discuss Pan-Africanist thinkers, Jamaican-born Black Nationalist Marcus Garvey should be referenced. Throughout WWI, Garvey fought for the cause of

African independence and highlighted the positive attributes of black people's collective past. Marcus Garvey and the Universal Negro Improvement Association (UNIA) formed a critical link in black America's centuries-long struggle for freedom, justice, and equality (The Marcus Garvey and U.N.I.A. Papers Project, UCLA). As the leader of the largest mass movement in Black history and forefather of the modern "black is beautiful" ideal; Garvey is also best known as a champion of the back to Africa movement. According to Garvey, the only path to economic independence and Black pride was the redemption of "Africa for the Africans".

Garvey also stated that Black men must organize the world over and build up for the race a mighty nation of their own in Africa (Holloway, Joseph). In August 1920, the Garvey movement was at its upmost. In New York City, 25,000 African-Americans attended a month-long convention. Black Nationalism and an African homeland were the focal points (Holloway, Joseph). Garvey felt the need of a home base in Africa. That home base would be the Republic of Liberia. Around that time, Liberia was in economic disarray because of corruption and mismanagement since its founding. Liberia's revenue was absent because the monies went into the pockets of the president and his associates. As a result, the country faced a national debt. Garvey knew that most of Africa were still under colonial rule. He also thought that Africans would need to be brought into the 20th century. Using Liberia as a base, Garvey proposed sending a few African-Americans (20,000 to 30,000 families at first) with skills, professions, and capital to settle in Liberia (Holloway, Joseph).

Liberia was the only independent Republic in West Africa at that time, was experiencing a financial crisis, and needed funds to pay off the national debt. Garvey discovered this was an opportunity to purchase land in Liberia. He offered the money in exchange for settlement of his people in Liberia. In 1920, Garvey had raised a $2million down payment to the government of Liberia to buy land for the resettlement of a small number of skilled blacks (Hollway Joseph). After the money had been raised, several teams of his representatives visited Liberia to lay the groundwork for his plan. Garvey then raised money to cancel Liberia's $5million international debt. Interestingly, President Charles D.B. King was already in Washington D.C. trying to get a $5million loan from the U.S. government.

On the other hand, Garvey sent an UNIA delegation of UNIA officials to complete the arrangements. While President King was in D.C. negotiating for a $5million loan, Dr. W.E.B Du Bois of the National Association for the Advancement of Colored People (NAACP) got himself appointed as Ambassador of the USA to attend the second inaugural in Liberia of President King. Soon after the New York world, along with every other major paper in New York City, as well as major black papers, was the recipient of a strange press release from the Liberian Consul General in the U.S. on July 10th (Grant, C. pg. 385-386). Once the press release was published, it effectively put an end to Marcus Garvey's settlement schemes in Africa. Due to this press release, no person or person's leaving the USA under the sponsorship of the Garvey movement in the USA will be allowed to land in the Republic of Liberia (Grant pg. 385-386).

Unfortunately, members of the UNIA who had settled in Liberia or were in route to the country were deported back to America. The truth is that DuBois convinced President King that Garvey wanted to overthrow the Liberian government. To add more fuel to the fire, Du Bois was working closely with the United States Department to destroy the UNIA in Liberia. He also had taken steps to hamper the UNIA and undermined Garvey's Liberian construction and resettlement plan (Holloway, J. E. 2010). The United States sent Du Bois to counter Garvey's settlement plan with an offer from firestone. It was believed that Du Bois played a significant role in the Liberian government refusal to receive the UNIA delegation. He also made the UNIA seem like a threat to the Americo-Liberian ruling group.

Dr. Dubois insisted that Garvey had a secret plan to take over the country, an actual plan in which he held. It is evident to say that the Black elite was jealous of Garvey's rise to power and tried to undermine his leadership (Holloway, J. E. 2010). Sadly, both Garvey and Du Bois had a natural dislike for each other based on class, caste, and color. It is stated, that the African-American groups are united by a common African ethnicity and culture; however, that is false. Many scholars fail to see the diversity in language, culture, class, and color among African-Americans and how those differences provided one group of African-Americans with extraordinary opportunities for higher educational and trade skills when compared to the overall black population (Holloway, J. E. 2010).

Historically, there has been animosity between Biracial and Black classes because of the association of fair skin with high statuses and class within the black social apex. Garvey recognized there was color stratification in America between fair and darker skin blacks and that he would save black America from itself by relocating the "true" sons and daughters of Africa back to their true homeland to create a United States of Africa.

On the contrary, the legacy of colorism discrimination by blacks against other blacks would destroy Garvey's movement (Holloway, Joseph). The harsh truth of the struggles between Du Bois and Garvey was that both were Pan-Africanist. Du Bois along with other black leaders worked with the US government to destroy the Pan- African movement as visualized by Garvey because he was not of their "caliber" he was seen inferior because of him being "dark skin," an Afro-Caribbean (West Indian), and a "foreigner." Both Garvey and Du Bois visions of Pan-Africanism clashed not over ideas or philosophy; however, undermined by notions of superiority or inferiority based on skin complexion (Holloway, Joseph). Garvey was the "Moses" of his people, and like the historic Moses, Garvey would lead his people to the promise land Liberia.

Modern day Pan Africanists

By the late 1940s, the African-American scholars of the movement had declined, with Africans now taking the lead of the movement. That was due in part to the leftist or communist sympathies of many Pan-Africanist advocates, as in the late 1940s and early '50s, the United States was in the midst of a Red Scare when Americans with communist affiliations or sympathies were actively persecuted and prosecuted (Pan Africanism 2016).

The prominent Pan-Africanist of this period was President Kwame Nkrumah of Ghana, who believed that European colonial rule of Africa, could be terminated if Africans could unite politically and economically. Nkrumah went on to be the front runner of the movement; for independence in Ghana, which came to fruition in 1957. The African-American brothers and sisters celebrated those developments in Africa. The Pan-African ideology resurfaced with renewed force in the United States from the late 1960s and '70s one manifestation of the Black Power movement. In the early 1970s, it had become quite common for African-Americans to explore their African cultural roots, adopt African form of cultural practice, particularly African styles of dress. In subsequent decades, perhaps the most prominent current of ideas that can be called Pan-Africanist. The Afrocentric movement, as espoused by such black intellectuals as Molefi Asante of Temple University, Cheikh Anta Diop of Senegal, the American historian Carter G. Woodson, and Maulana Ron Karenga, the creator of Kwanzaa (Pan Africanism 2016).

Since the 1960s, Afrocentrism continued to gain popularity in the United States during the 1980s. The movement highlights African forms of thought and culture as a counteractive to the long tradition of European cultural and intellectual domination.

HIDDEN COMMONALITIES REVEALED

"The more you know of your history, the more liberated you are."

~Dr. Maya Angelou~

AFRICAN INFLUENCE IN THE BLACK/ AFRICAN DIASPORA COMMUNITIES

HIDDEN COMMONALITIES

Chapter 3

CUISINE

While researching Black/African history, African Diaspora may be a new term for many people. It may not often be used in conversations or writing. Although the African diaspora refers simply to Africans aboard who live outside their ancestral continent, predominantly to the Americas, Europe, the Middle East, Asia, and among other areas around the globe. However, historically, African diaspora is the term commonly used to describe the mass dispersion of peoples from Africa during the Transatlantic Slave Trades, from the 1500s to the 1800s.

This Diaspora took millions of people from Western and Central Africa to different regions throughout the Americas and the Caribbean (African Diaspora Cultures | Oldways). The African ancestors landed in regions that featured different local foods and cuisines, and other cultural influences that molded their distinctive cooking styles. The overall pattern of a plant-based, colorful diet based on vegetables, fruits, tubers and grains, nuts, healthy oils and seafood (where available) was shared throughout Africa and the African diaspora regions (North America, Caribbean, and Latin America). But, their cultural peculiarities have a reason to be celebrated (African Diaspora Cultures | Oldways). Their scrumptious tastes can be shared and tried by people worldwide.

"Mama Africa" is the habitat to leafy greens, root vegetables, mashed tubers and beans, and varieties of plant crops across its lands. In Central and Western Africa, traditional meals were often based on hearty vegetable soups and stews, meats, seafood, full of spices and aromas, poured over boiled and mashed tubers or grains. In Eastern Africa, whole grains and vegetables are the highlights of traditional meals, especially cabbage, kale and maize (cornmeal). On the other hand in the Horn of Africa, where Ethiopia and Somalia are found, traditional meals are based on flat bread like injera (made out of teff, sorghum or whole wheat) and beans blended with spices, like lentils, fava beans and chickpeas (African Diaspora Cultures | Oldways).

Currently, many meals in the Horn are still prepared in halal style meaning they include no pork, no alcohol, and meat only from animals who have died on their own. Across Africa, couscous, sorghum, millet, and rice were enjoyed as the bases of meals, or as porridges and sides. Watermelon and okra are both native to Africa, and many believe that cucumbers are too. Beans were eaten in abundance everywhere, especially black-eyed peas, which were often pounded into a powder for tasty bean pastes seared as fritters (African Diaspora Cultures /Oldways).

African influence in Southern United States Cuisine

The influence of Southern foods comes directly from colonial and antebellum slave quarters. Southern food, often recognized as the ideal American cuisine, originated from a complex blend of European, Native American, and African origins that found realization in the hands of enslaved people (Regelski, C 2015). While Southern food has evolved from sources and cultures of diverse regions, classes, races, and ethnicities; it is apparent that Africans and their descendants have one of the strongest yet least recognized roles in southern cuisines.

For Africans, cooking was about culture and community as much it was about survival. Through the horrors of the Middle Passage and captivity in North America, generations of slaves preserved and created culinary traditions that remain strong today. Southern food reminds Americans of this difficult past, but it can also help us understand it and respect it (Regelski, C 2015). Africans were accustomed to large quantities of greens and vegetables in their diet, so their descendants featured these sorts of foods into the daily fare of their masters. Some historians state that adding such vitamin- and mineral-rich food plants saved masters and their families from nutritional deficiencies.

The diet in Africa was centered around stews served over a starchy base such as rice; or "fufu," a pounded mass of boiled yams, cassava, plantain or millet. The effect of this food inspired Louisiana-style cookery in which chicken or seafood is served with a sauce over a bed of rice. Cajun dishes such as gumbo and jambalaya also show an African influence (Mitchell, P 1993). The dish Jambalaya is an offspring of Spanish paella and Jollof rice a West African delicacy. There is a variation between rural style jambalaya and also New Orleans style Jambalaya. In rural Louisiana, jambalaya is brown because the rice in the dish absorbs the sauce in which it is cooked.

By tradition, it is cooked in cast-iron pots due to the high temperature the pot has while cooking (Bienvenu, M. 2011). As a result, there is a complete caramelization of natural sugars in meats and vegetables. The brown coloring is then absorbed by the rice. In New Orleans, Jambalaya is usually red because of the heavy use of tomatoes. New Orleans Jambalaya is an outgrowth of jollof rice. Also, jollof rice is related to paella because the ingredients include whatever is available; however, tomatoes and rice are major ingredients. Like paella and jambalaya, the entire dish of jollof rice is prepared in a single pot (Bienvenu, M. 2011).

The West African influence is also particularly strong throughout the low-county region of the Carolinas, Georgia, and Florida (Gullah/Geechee nation) cuisine. The ingredients include grains and vegetables that define the low-country, as well as cowpeas and black-eyed peas, okra, greens, rice, watermelon, yams in which are staples of the West African diet likewise sorghum and sesame (benne). Also, Africans were fond of deep frying and grilling. Carolinians also adopted the African cooking techniques such as one-pot cooking, stews, gumbos, thickening with okra or nuts. Africans and their descendants prepared greens by laying meat on top too, and without that influence, the southern tradition of using smoked meats as seasoning may never have begun (Moss, R. F. 2013).

African influence in the Caribbean (West Indian) Cuisine

The West Indies and Caribbean Islands bring tropical accents and various seafood to the African Heritage Diet Pyramid. Approximately 23 million people of African descent live in the Caribbean (African Diaspora Cultures | Oldways). Throughout the Caribbean, we find the fusion of African, Native American, European, East Indian, Arab and Chinese cuisines. These traditions were brought from many countries when they came to the Caribbean. Also, the population has created styles that are exclusive to the region. Surrounded by ocean, traditional African-Caribbean fare included a variety of seafood, like salt fish and conch; tropical fruits, like papaya and guava; rice and peas dishes, typically featuring pigeon peas or red beans. Coconut milk, breadfruit, callaloo (leafy greens), calalou(okra), yams, plantains, ackee, annatto, and pumpkins are all found in the Caribbean islands. In the southern parts of the Caribbean, roti is a popular flatbread, primarily made from whole wheat. flour, that can be filled with curried vegetables and shrimp, or bean dishes, as a warm, soft roll-up (African Diaspora Cultures | Oldways).

A popular dish that shows evidence of an African influence is Haitian Gumbo/Kalalou(Okra). The name gumbo is likely derived from the African Bantu dialect word Kigombo. In resemblance with Kalalou Gumbo, there is Louisiana style Gumbo. This dish also has an African influence or even a connection to the Choctaw Native American tribe. Due to Haiti and Louisiana's French influence, the dishes may have been inspired by Bouillabaisse a traditional fish stew originating from Marseille, France (Tucker, S. 2009). What makes Haitian Gumbo, as well Louisiana Creole Gumbo alike are the use of okra and tomatoes. The tomatoes create a red coloring in the dishes. It is believed that both dishes are the reinterpretation of traditional African cooking. West Africans used the vegetable okra as a base for many dishes, including soups, often pairing okra with meat and shrimp, salt and pepper as seasonings (Bienvenu, M., Brasseaux, C. A., & Brasseaux, R. A. 2005). Due to the African influence in both dishes is why the gumbo dishes are superb.

Origin of African Fufu and its influence in the Caribbean

Fufu (foofoo, fufuo, foufou) is a core food with profound roots in Ghana's history and communal in many countries of West Africa and the Caribbean (Nweke, F. I.). It is often made with cassava flour. Other flours, such as semolina, maize flour or mashed plantains may take the place of cassava flour. Fufu is normally served alongside soup. An alternative method is to boil starchy food crops like cassava, yams or plantains and cocoyams and then pound them into a dough-like consistency (Gibbon, E. 2005).

A similar staple in the African Great Lakes region is ugali. It is customarily made from maize flour (masa) and is also eaten in Southern Africa. The name gali is used to refer to the dish in Kenya and Tanzania. Other dishes related to fufu are called nshima in Zambia, nsima in Malawi, sadza in Zimbabwe, pap in South Africa, posho in Uganda, luku, fufu, nshima, moteke, semoule, ugali and bugari in Republic of the Congo and in the Democratic Republic of the Congo and phaletshe in Botswana (Gibbon, E. 2005).

Caribbean nations with great populations of African origin like Cuba, Dominican Republic, Haiti, and Puerto Rico, use yucca (cassava), or yams and mash them with other delectable ingredients to make fufu. Interestingly, Cuba maintains its original African stem name, termed simply as fufú or with added descriptive extensions like fufú de platano (plantain fufu) or fufú de platano pintón (mashed plantain fufu) (Wheatley, C., Scott, G. J., Best, R., & Wiersema, S.

pg.17). In other islands, fufu goes by the names of mangú (mashed plantains) in the Dominican Republic and mofongo in Puerto Rico. What differentiates Caribbean "fufú" from its West African ancestor is a denser texture with stronger flavors.

As oppose to fufu from Cuba, other islands fufú's core is less gelatinous dough and more of a consistent mass (Martinez, D., & Styler, C. 2005). The Puerto Rican mofongo depicts the Creole Caribbean trend toward the fufú's higher density and robust seasoning. Although mofongo has a conspicuous African character, the dish has also adopted styles from Taino Native Americans and the Iberian Peninsula (Spain and Portugal), to create a dish containing exclusively plantains. To prepare mofongo, plantains are deep-fried; however not to the point as tostones (fried plantain). Following, they are mashed with broth, garlic, and olive oil. The lump from the mashed plantain is then pressed and rounded into a crusty orb. Next, meat usually chicharrón (pork), is then stuffed into the chunky ball of browned plantains. Some mofongo recipes call for meat or vegetable salsa criolla" (related to American Creole sauce) poured on top of the hot sphere. While other recipes like "mofongo relleno" uses seafood for the dish. On the other hand, traditional mofongo, consist of seasoned and stuffed with meat and bathed in a chicken broth soup (Garth, H. 2012).

Another relative of fufu is Cou-cou(coo-coo) or Fungi, makes up part of the national dishes of Antigua and Barbuda,

Barbados, British Virgin Islands and the U.S. Virgin Islands. It consists mainly of cornmeal (corn flour) and okra (ochroes) (Barrow, E.; Lee, K. 1988). Fufu is usually part of or added to a soupy sauce, or on the side with a soupy dish. Cou-cou was a regular meal for enslaved Africans brought over to Barbados. Furthermore, cou-cou serves as Barbados national dish and is prepared with fried or steamed flying fish, or even corned beef or beef stew. Similarly, Antigua's fufu also serves as part of the national dish; however, it's called fungi/fungee and is made using cornmeal and okra (Barrow, E.; Lee, K. 1988). And in Haiti, fufu is called tomtom. It is mostly made of breadfruit but can be made of plantain, cornmeal, or yams, and is usually served with an okra based stew or soup (Yurnet-Thomas, M. 2002).

African influence in South (Latin) American Cuisine

There are roughly 100 million people of African descent living in South America, with a majority of the population in Brazil. The similar African Heritage staple-dishes such as soups and stews, rice and beans, and tubers like yucca and cassava are also in South America. Okra, peanuts, squashes and plantains appear in many dishes, as well as fruits and fruit juices like mangoes and guava (African Diaspora Cultures | Oldways). Some of the popular ingredients are red snapper, avocado, cilantro, and tapioca. Native American influences are seen in South Americans corn/maize use, and their tamales that combine peas, carrots, potatoes, rice, and various spices as fillings. Moqueca Baiana is a popular traditional dish of Brazil. It is a seafood stew with prominent African roots due to using palm oil, coconut milk, shrimp and crab, onions, garlic, peppers, tomatoes, and cilantro (African Diaspora Cultures | Oldways).

Indigenous African and Southern United States influence in Liberian Cuisine

Liberian cuisine has been inspired by the United States particularly foods from the American South (Southern or Soul food) due to the repatriation of freed Blacks from the south to Liberia. The cuisine is also intertwined with traditional African foods. A Liberian dish like sautéed collard greens captures the connection between freed blacks and indigenous people of Liberia. Depending on your liking Liberian style collard greens includes seafood (fish, shrimp, and crabs), meat (pig feet, pork, and beef) or poultry (turkey and chicken). However, habanero or scotch bonnet peppers gives the dish its key flavor. The Liberian diet is also centered on the consumption of rice and other starches, tropical fruits, vegetables, and local seafood and meat. Liberia also has a tradition of baking imported from the United States that is unique in West Africa (The Baking Recipes of Liberia). Some of the baked dishes include banana rice bread (which was likely created by Liberian indigenous people), corn bread and short bread biscuit (which originated from the American south).

Chapter 4

MUSIC AND DANCE

African influence on the African diaspora music genres

African music

Traditionally, the music of Africa is historically ancient, rich and with various regions and nations of Africa having many diverse musical traditions. Throughout Africa, music has been passed down orally (or aurally) and is not written. African music heavily relies on percussion instruments of every variety, involving xylophones, drums, and tone-producing instruments such as the mbira or "thumb piano." Traditional African music is performed with functional intent in celebrations, festivals, and storytelling (Definitions of Styles and Genres: Traditional and Contemporary African Music). North Africa and the Horn of Africa

Music of the Nile valley and Horn of Africa has close ties with Middle Eastern music and uses similar melodic scales. North African music has an extensive range from music of ancient Egypt, Berber, and Tuareg music of the desert nomads (Abdullahi, M. D. 2001). Along with the North African style of music, there is music from Sudan, Eritrea, Ethiopia, Djibouti, and Somalia. Somali music is typically pentatonic, using five pitches per octave in contrast to a heptatonic (seven note) scale such as the major scale (Abdullahi, M. D. 2001). The music of the Ethiopian highlands uses a fundamental modal system called qenet, of which there are four main modes: tezeta, bati, ambassel, and anchihoy. Three additional modes are variations on the above: tezeta minor, bati major, and bati minor (Shelemay, K. K. 2001).

West, Central, Southeast and South Africa

Ethnomusicological pioneer Arthur Morris Jones (1889–1980) detected that the shared rhythmic principles of Sub-Saharan African music traditions constitute one main system (Ladzekpo, C. K. 1996). Correspondingly, master drummer and scholar C. K. Ladzekpo affirms the "profound homogeneity" of sub-Saharan African rhythmic principles (Ladzekpo, C. K. 1996). By tradition, African music is frequently functional in nature. Normally, performances are long often involving the participation of the audience. For instance, there are songs and dances that accompany childbirth, marriage, hunting and political activities, to ward off evil spirits and to pay respects to good spirits, the dead and the ancestors. Each music is performed by professional musicians, based on sacral music or ceremonial and courtly music performed at royal courts.

Musicologically, Sub-Saharan Africa may be divided into four regions (Jones, A. M. 1978):

The eastern region includes the music of Uganda, Kenya, Rwanda, Burundi, Tanzania, Malawi, Mozambique and Zimbabwe and the islands of Madagascar, the Seychelles, Mauritius, and Comor. Many of these have been influenced by Arabic music and also by the music of India, Indonesia, and Polynesia, though the region's indigenous musical traditions are primarily in the mainstream of the sub-Saharan Niger–Congo-speaking peoples.

The southern region includes the music of South Africa, Lesotho, Swaziland, Botswana, Namibia, and Angola. The central region includes the music of Chad, the Central African Republic, the Democratic Republic of the Congo and Zambia, including Pygmy music.

West African music includes the music of Senegal and the Gambia, of Guinea and Guinea-Bissau, Sierra Leone and Liberia, of the inland plains of Mali, Niger and Burkina Faso, the coastal nations of Cote d'Ivoire, Ghana, Togo, Benin, Nigeria, Cameroon, Gabon and the Republic of the Congo and islands such as Sao Tome and Principe. Southern, Central, and West Africa are similarly in the broad Sub-Saharan musical tradition, but draw their ancillary influences primarily from Western Europe and North America.

African Influence on North American (African-American) Music

African-American (Black American) music traces to the polyrhythmic music of the ethnic groups of Africa, exclusively to Western, Sahelian, and Sub-Saharan regions. African oral traditions encouraged the use of music to pass on history, teach lessons, ease suffering, and relay messages during chattel slavery. The African pedigree of African-American music is clear in some common elements such as call and response, syncopation, percussion, improvisation, swung notes, blue notes, the use of falsetto, melisma, and complex multi-part harmony (Papa M.Gerber A. and Mohamed A.).

Throughout slavery, Africans in America combined traditional European hymns with African elements to create spirituals (Stewart, E. L. 1998). Within the African-American community, "Lift Every Voice and Sing" in addition to the American national anthem, "The Star-Spangled Banner," are sung or in lieu of it. The composers of the 1900 "Lift Every Voice and Sing" are James Weldon Johnson and John Rosamond Johnson. The song is to be performed for the birthday of Abraham Lincoln. The song was and continues to be, a popular way for African-Americans to recall past struggles and express ethnic solidarity, faith, and hope for the future (Bond, J., & Wilson, S. K. 2000). The song was adopted as the "Negro National Anthem" by the NAACP in 1919 (Bond, J., & Wilson, S. K. 2000). During events hosted by African-American churches, schools, and other organizations, "Lift Ev'ry Voice and Sing" traditionally is sung immediately following, or instead of, "The Star-Spangled Banner" (McIntyre, D.B. 2000).

Because of the blackface minstrel show, African-American music entered mainstream American society in the 19th century. In the early 20th century, numerous musical forms with origins in the African-American community had renovated American popular music. Ministered by the technological novelties of radio and phonograph records, ragtime, jazz, blues, and swing also became popular overseas, and the 1920s became known as the Jazz Age. The early 20th century also presented the creation of the first African-American Broadway shows, films such as King Vidor's Hallelujah!, and operas such as George Gershwin's Porgy and Bess.

Music genres like Rock and Roll, Doo Wop, Soul, and Rhythm and Blues(R&B) developed in the mid-20th century. These genres became very popular in White audiences and were influences for other genres such as Surf. In the turn of the 1970s, an urban African-American tradition of using rhyming slang to bash one's enemies (or friends), as well as the West Indian tradition of toasting grew into a new form of music. In the South Bronx (New York City) the spoken or chanting rhythmic street talk of "Rapping" grew into the hugely successful cultural force known as Hip Hop (RM Hip Hop Magazine 1986).

Although hip-hop would become a multicultural movement, it remained important to many African-Americans. The African-American Cultural Movement of the 1960s and 1970s also stimulated the growth of funk and later hip-hop forms such as rap, house, new jack swing, and go-go. House music originated in black communities in Chicago in the 1980s. African-American music has experienced far more widespread acceptance in American popular music in the 21st century than ever before. In addition to creating newer forms of African-American music, modern artists have also started a rebirth of older genres in genres such as neo-soul and modern funk-inspired songs (Southern, E. 1997).

In respect to African-American dance and dances from the Caribbean Islands and Latin America; they find its earliest roots from hundreds of African ethnic groups merged with European dances, forming the extension of the African aesthetic in the Americas. By tradition, dance has always been essential to daily life in Africa. Throughout the Americas, dance has also helped enslaved Africans connect with their homeland, as a result keeping their cultural traditions alive (The New York Public Library African-American desk reference 1999).

Before enslavement, Africans danced for special occasions, such as a birth or marriage; or even for day-day activities to have an outlook for a better future. African-

Americans (Black Americans) sang and danced while working as slaves and as they converted to the religions of the Americas and incorporated their African traditions into these religions. Africans who worked in the Caribbean and Latin America were given more freedom to dance than enslaved Africans in North America (The New York Public Library African-American desk reference. 1999). Unfortunately, many North American slave masters prohibited Africans from most forms of dancing. So, Africans got around the prohibition of dancing in the fields. For instance, since lifting the feet was considered dancing, many dances included foot shuffling and hip and torso movement. Dances popular in the 18th century include ring shout or ring dance, the calenda, chica, and juba (The New York Public Library African-American desk reference 1999).

In the 19th century, African-American dance appeared in minstrel shows. These shows often presented African-Americans as caricatures for ridicule to large audiences. The first African-American dance to become popular with white dancers was the cakewalk in 1891(Cakewalk Dance). Dances that later followed in this tradition include the Charleston, the Lindy Hop, the Jitterbug and the swing (Malnig, J pg.19-23,2009). In the Harlem Renaissance period, African-American Broadway shows such as Shuffle Along helped to establish and legitimize African-American dancers. Dance forms like tap which is a combination of African and European influences gained widespread popularity thanks to dancers such as Bill Robinson and were also used by leading White choreographers, who often hired African-American dancers (Malnig, J pg.19-23,2009). Contemporary African-American dance is descended from these earlier dance forms and also has ties to African and Caribbean dance forms. Groups such as the Alvin Ailey American Dance Theater have continued to contribute to the growth of this form. Modern popular dance in America is also deeply influenced by African-American dance. Modern dance in America has also presented many influences from African-American dance most notably in the hip-hop genre (The New York Public Library African American desk reference. 1999)

African Influence on Caribbean and Latin Music

Musical genres of the Latin American region range in various forms. Each genre is fused of African, European, Asian, and Indigenous American influences. However, the genres of the region were largely created by descendants of enslaved Africans ex. Afro-Caribbean Music and Afro-Latin Music, with contributions from East Indian descendants who created Indo-Caribbean Music or Chutney. The styles of music that gained its popularity outside the region include Soca, Calypso, Reggae, Kompa, Reggaeton, Merengue, Samba, Tango, Latin Jazz, Zouk, Bachata, Salsa, and Punta. Although there are musical commonalities among the Caribbean, Central and

South America there is language barriers within the music. Based on colonialism there is a strong influence of Spanish, English, French, and Dutch throughout the region.

Calypso is a genre of music that originated in Trinidad and Tobago and is mainly of African origin. The genre traces to the traditions of West Africans regarding music, structure, and function. Interestingly, Calypso has been called a poor man's newspaper, due to the illiteracy during those times. Calypso also traces its roots to African traditions of improvised songs of self-praise and scorn for others. It then became both a dance and cultural record of events at first in single tone style with implicit meanings and a spicy flavor (The National Carnival Commission of Trinidad and Tobago).

The root of Calypso comes in various forms. Some say it came from "kaiso" a Hausa word for "bravo." Others say the word came from the French "carrousseaux" a drinking party; or the Spanish "calliso" a tropical song; or even the Carib "carieto", also means a tropical song (The National Carnival Commission of Trinidad and Tobago). The first wave of professional calypso singers or calypsonians became known as the Old Bridgade, including singers such as Growling Tiger, Lord Beginner, Atilla the Hun, the Roaring Lion and Lord Pretender. By 1945, other wave of singers rose to meet the demand for more entertaining songs. This Young Brigade included Lord Kitchener, Mighty Spoiler, Mighty Dictator and Lord Wonder, and later the Mighty Sparrow.

During the Black Power movement in the 1970s, a new generation of singers such as Black Stalin and Brother Valentino came to part. Musicians such as Shadow, Maestro, Merchant and Explainer, ushered a broad range of voices and musical styles. Then in 1978, Lady calypsonian Calypso Rose was the first woman to win the Calypso Monarch competition. Calypso Rose also paved the way for many more women on the Calypso stage. Over the years, the calypso art form has been transformed and presented in various categories the major ones being; Political Commentary, Social Commentary, Humorous, Soca, Ragga Soca, Chutney Soca and Nation Building (The National Carnival Commission of Trinidad and Tobago).

Soca "Sokah" (soul of Calypso) is a Caribbean music genre that originated in Trinidad and Tobago in the late 1970s and developed into a range of styles in the 1980s-Present. Soca is an offspring of calypso music and is used for dancing carnival and at fetes (party). Many musicians from Anglophone Caribbean countries like Barbados, Guyana, Grenada, Saint Lucia, Antigua and Barbuda, US Virgin Islands, British Virgin Islands, The Bahamas, Saint Kitts and Nevis, Jamaica, Belize, and Montserrat have also helped to mold soca music in the past 20 years (Dudley, S). The creation of Soca music is credited to Garfield Blackman, a.k.a. Lord Shorty. Blackman sang Calypso, a type of Afro-Trinidadian song style characterized by storytelling and verbal wit. According to Blackman, soca music is a fusion of Calypso and East Indian music. Soca music also reflects Trinidad's two largest ethnic group which is East Indian and African descendants (Dudley, S).

One of the most popular music and dance styles ever to emerge from Brazil is the Samba. Samba evolved in Rio de Janeiro by the early 20th century and grew to become the quintessential music and dance from associated with Rio's Carnival (Sambassadors of groove).

The word "Samba" is thought to be derived from the Kimbundu (Angolan) term samba, which means invitation to dance. The dance was also a common appellation for the dance parties held by slaves and former slaves in the rural areas of Rio. These dances involved gyrating hip movements (called umbigada) and had roots going back to the colonial period in the Congolese and Angolan circle dances (Sambassadors of groove). As a song form, samba was extremely popular during the turn of the century, with some of the early recordings dating back to 1911.

Brazilian crooners and composers put samba on the international radar, and icons such as Carmen Miranda embraced the form, becoming a star in Brazil long before her move to the U.S. and Hollywood as a personification of Brazil's exuberant side (Sambassadors of groove). By the 1950s, as samba-canção began to lose its drive, a more percussive and funkier style of samba emerged in the poor areas and shantytowns (known as favelas).

Throughout the 1970s, samba saw its rise within the era of MPB (música popular Brasileira) as artists such as Milton Nascimento, Djavan, and Ivan Lins modernized the more dynamic batucada style with contemporary harmony and instrumentation. They infused samba with rock, jazz, and other forms, and bringing the style into the mainstream (Sambassadors of groove). Even though much of samba's history is centered in Rio de Janeiro, a new development of the genre began to emerge in the eastern state of Bahia in the 1980s, as artists in Salvador created a new percussive style that was a bit slower and more driving, with lyrics that reflected the ideology of Brazil's African Diaspora (Sambassadors of groove).

The group Olodum pioneered by the bloco Afro style, which reformed some of the batucada elements of Rio's samba and focused on a more hypnotic, drum-infused sound. Olodum's lyrics spoke of black culture and pride. Olodum also gave the Bahian youth an outlet for their frustrations through the formation of a strong community organization by providing education and opportunity (Sambassadors of groove). With much of Brazil's black youth on the fringe of society, Olodum provided much needed cultural and political refuge. The group produced one of Brazil's most exciting new samba offshoots. Eventually, the bloco-Afro sound would fuse with Jamaican reggae and be known as samba-reggae, resulting in one of the most popular embodiments of samba into the 21st century (Sambassadors of groove).

The Western Influence on African Popular Music

Contemporary African music is also highly diverse; however, it shares many characteristics of Western popular music in the mid-twentieth-century. Beginning with recording technology and developing the recording industry, contemporary African music has been heavily influenced by Rhythm and Blues, Jazz, Funk, American soul music, Jamaican Reggae, Zouk, Hip Hop, and other musical forms from the Americas (Definitions of Styles and Genres: Traditional and Contemporary African Music).

One of the most important 20th-century singers of South African popular music was Miriam Makeba, who played a key-role, in the 60s, in drawing global audience's attention to African music and its meaning. Another prominent person who helped to form Contemporary African music was Fela Kuti. Kuti invented the famous music genre name Afrobeat in Accra, Ghana in 1968 (Grass, R. F. 1986). Afro beat, is the most popular form of music in Nigeria, Ghana, some parts of Africa and the world. Afro beat combines traditional Ghana music, jazz, highlife, funk, and chanted vocals, fused with percussion and vocal styles (Grass, R. F. 1986).

Music Genre such as Highlife, originated in Ghana at the turn of the 20th century and incorporated the traditional harmonic 9th, and melodic and the main rhythmic structures in traditional Akan music, and married them with Western instruments (Oti, S. 2009). This genre has a combination of North American, West African and Latin American styles. Highlife eventually emerged in the 1950s in Sierra Leone and Liberia. Highlife has been popular especially among the Liberian Kru people, who were sailors that played Spanish guitar, banjo, pennywhistle, harmonica, accordion, mandolin and concertina (Oti, S. 2009).

In the 21st century, afro beats have become a largely different style combining influences from Congolese rumba, hip-hop, and dancehall. Early hits included "African Queen" by 2face Idibia (2004) and "No One like You" by P-Square (2007) (How Nigeria's Afrobeats are redefining the sound of Africa 2014). Recently, the Azonto style of dance from Ghana has become closely associated with Afrobeats, and more up-tempo songs have become popular. Later hits also include "Bumper2Bumper" by Wande Coal (2008), "Oleku" by Ice Prince (2010) and "Kukere" by Iyanya (2011). Afrobeats have gained mainstream recognition outside of Africa, especially within the UK. Afrobeats nightclubs are now primary features of UK's nightlife with clubs opening in most major cities (How Nigeria's Afrobeats are redefining the sound of Africa 2014).

Liberian Music has taken a new dimension with the new Hipco artists changing the style of music. Hipco (Co for short) is the combination of Hiphop and Colloquial (Giamo, C. 2011). Colloquial or Liberian Kreyol (English based Creole) which is a vernacular speech, the style of communication with which Liberians speak and relate to each other. The genre evolved in the 1980s and has always been socially and politically bent. In the 1990s, it continued to develop through the civil wars, and today stands as a definitive mark of Liberian culture (Giamo, C. 2011). The Hipco artists are, Takun J, Lukay Buckey, Sundaygar Dearboy, Bucky Raw, Nyae Slanger, Raw Pekin, and much more.

Chapter 5

LANGUAGE

Enslaved Africans were drawn from a large range of societies and cultures. Although Europeans described them simply as "Africans", African people regarded themselves according to kinship groups, lineage, and ethnicity. Distinct traditions and languages also defined each ethnic group. As a result, those belonging to unique groups, lineage, and ethnicities inclined to see others as "foreigners" (The Colonial Williamsburg Foundation 2017). Europeans beginning in the fifteenth century introduced the language of race (The Colonial Williamsburg Foundation 2017).

It was significant to understand the language of European and Americans, Slave traders and plantation owners for the enslaved because that legally determined so many aspects of their lives. Therefore, a new pidgin language evolved, which was developed from the language used by early Portuguese sailors and African traders along the West and Central Coast (The Colonial Williamsburg Foundation 2017).

In the Americas, new languages emerged and evolved. The language styles derived from the Africanization of European languages. The languages are identified as creole, patois, or pidgin and in the United States, Black English, African-American English, or Ebonics (McLaren, J. pg.97).

Creole languages have resulted from the interactions between speakers of non-standard varieties of European languages and speakers of non-European languages (Mufwene, S.S). Due to creole languages developing in the colonies, they are mainly based on English, French, Portuguese and Spanish (Mufwene, S.S.) The varieties of creole language include Haitian Creole, Louisiana Creole, Antillean Creole French (Martinique, Guadeloupe, and Dominica), and Guianan Creole, in which French is the lexifier (Mufwene, S.S). English is the lexifier to English-based creole languages such as: Barbadian (Bajan) Creole, Jamaican Patois, Trinidadian Creole, Gullah (on the Sea Islands of the southeastern United States), Bahamian Creole, Guyanese Creole, and Leeward Caribbean Creole English (Antigua and Barbuda, Montserrat, Saint Kitts, and Nevis) (Mufwene, S.S).

The creole language also emerged in Africa. Some creole languages include Sierra Leonean Krio, Nigerian Creole (Nigerian Pidgin), Liberian Kreyol (Liberian English), Ghanaian Pidgin English, which derived from the English language (Mufwene, S.S). A language such as Mauritian Creole is French based. Sango, a creole based on the Ngbandi language and spoken in the Central African Republic; Kinubi, based on the Arabic language and spoken in Uganda. Kikongo-Kituba and Lingala are based on Kikongo-Kimanyanga and Bobangi, respectively, and are spoken in both the Democratic Republic of the Congo and the Republic of the Congo (Mufwene, S.S).

In respect to the literary world, Africanized English is a recognized literary element found in the works of celebrated creative writers, whose skill in using vernacular has often earned them considerable literary acknowledgment. Although it is a trademark of African diasporic literature, Africanized English has become a controversial social and political issue, relating to the dilemma of identity, as shown in the 1996 controversy surrounding the use of Ebonics as a teaching tool in the Oak land, California, school system (McLaren, J. pg.97). While studying the Ebonics debate, it may be seen as a local issue, but on a deeper level, the controversy suggests a range of problematic literary, cultural, social, and political issues relevant to literary production in the African Diaspora (McLaren, J. pg.97).

Ebonics developed as a response to the post-civil rights era and the dilemmas faced by school systems was mandated to "educate" African-American youth, and, it was believed, students had difficulty learning Standard English because of Ebonics (McLaren, J. pg.98). The analysis of black language patterns was inherently political; educators such as Robert L. Williams and Geneva Smitherman were engaged in a cultural battle and not simply a pedagogical debate over the effective teaching of English. Williams's edited collection Ebonics: The True Language of Black Folks (1975) helped to popularize the term Ebonics; Smitherman's "Talkin and Testifyin": The Language of Black America (1977) valorized Ebonics and examined the origins of Africanized English especially in the African-American context (McLaren, J. pg.98). Ebonics refers to the language of West African, Caribbean, and North American slave descendant of African origin. Ebonics includes the various idioms, patois, argots, idiolects, and social dialects of black people (McLaren, J. pg.98). Labels such as nonstandard and broken English directed to Ebonics were derogatory and reflected "some degree of white bias" (McLaren, J. pg.98).

Ebonics has become an element in literature of the diaspora, and a sign of the actual language patterns spoken by characters in fictional works or by the "speakers" in poetic discourse (McLaren, J. pg.98). There is a clear discrepancy between its negation on a social-political level by certain black and white spokespersons and its valorization by literary artists and linguists (McLaren, J. pg. 98). The author of "Talkin and Testifyin" asserts that African-American language styles are derived from patterns found in certain West African languages. Smitherman also states there are direct relationships between Caribbean English and West African pidgin, predominantly of Jamaica and Nigeria, and that both forms respectively "provide a kind of linguistic mirror image of Black American (Pidgin and Creole) English (McLaren, J. pg.98).

Also, linguist and Kiswahili specialist Abdul Nanji points out the influences on Ebonics which include Bantu languages of Central and East Africa. Structural elements of languages from these regions can also be located in Ebonics. Nanji also traces the relationship between African languages and diaspora languages because of the way African languages are structured (McLaren, J. pg.98).

Nanji describes how the languages are set-up from the central part of Africa, Congo, and to East Africa, Kenya, Tanzania, Uganda, Rwanda, Burundi, Malawi, the northern part of Mozambique, and Angola (McLaren, J. pg.99). Nanji goes on to say that, there is a cluster of one language tree or family. During slavery, Africans were able to preserve their cultures, and these cultures were not ruined by the imposition of European cultures. The base of African culture is still there, and you find the carryover in the language. There has also been "cross-fertilization" involving Ebonics, hip-hop, and contemporary African popular culture, Nanji addresses (McLaren, J. pg.99).

Last, while in a literary sense, Standard English has been manipulated by numerous creative writers of the diaspora and the African continent. Ali A. Mazrui states that "creative writers like Chinua Achebe have helped the trend towards the Africanization of English." In comparison to Achebe, Africanized English has been written by, Cyprian Ekwensi, Ken

Saro-Wiwa, Wole Soyinka, Derek Walcott, Kamau Brathwaite, Merle Hodge, Patricia Powell, Langston Hughes, Amiri Baraka, Sonia Sanchez, August Wilson, Ntozake Shange, Toni Morrison, and Gayl Jones (McLaren, J. pg.99). Throughout the United States, the move to erase Africanized language suggests an underlying critique of African survivals and the dilemma of identity (McLaren, J. pg.100).

BUILDING BLACK SOLIDARITY WORLD–WIDE

"African peoples, both on the continent and in the diaspora, share not merely a common history, but a common destiny"

~The Pan-African Ideology~

HIDDEN COMMONALITIES

Chapter 6

MYTHS AND STEREOTYPES OF AFRICANS AND AFRICAN DESCENDANTS

Africans, African-Americans, Afro-Caribbeans, and Afro-Latinos/Latinas are united by their common ancestry. They are also connected due to the history of oppression under their European conquerors. Africans and African descendants differ because they have been shaped by different historical experiences and environments. However, they are all African people. This has been argued by the likes of Kwame Nkrumah, WEB Dubois, Marcus Garvey, Malcolm X, and many others. Even Nelson Mandela said in his speech before an African-American audience in Harlem, NY that, "We are all children of Africa" (Mwakikagile, G. pg.36).

Although there are a common identity and history of oppression, relations between Africans, African-Americans, and Afro-Caribbeans has not always been a good one. Unfortunately, many do not always see themselves as the same despite their African heritage (Mwakikagile, G. pg. 36). They constitute distinct ethnic groups in countries such as the United States, Canada, England, the Caribbean and Latin America. They have shared negative depiction toward each other (Mwakikagile, G. pg. 36). Those depictions have also been shaped not only by their historical experiences; however also by their conquerors who have played a key role using various means including miseducation and the media to keep them divided (Mwakikagile, G. pg. 36). As a whole, Blacks have always been a group to be mocked, stereotyped, and stigmatized by society. In this chapter, I intend to focus on the way Blacks view themselves.

African stereotypes

African stereotypes are one of the most negative around the world. The continent's attention has been about wars, poverty, or HIV/AIDS. At times, Africa is depicted as a country. However, it is a diverse continent with 54 countries and thousands of ethnic groups. Unfortunately, neighboring African countries have negative connotations about each other as well. Also, all black Africans resemble is a common stereotype. For instance, it is believed that all Africans are dark skin, with broad noses and full lips. Even though there is nothing, wrong with these physical traits, Africans have various features, skin tones, and hair textures. You cannot always assume that a specific African region has a distinct look also. Another stereotype is Africa being all jungle. This notion stems from the television stations such as the discovery channel and the national geographic magazine, which only show savannahs and wildlife. There are urban areas throughout Africa as well (Kelland, Z. 2014).

African (Black) American Stereotypes

Although much has changed since the days of Sambo, Jim Crow, the Savage, Mammy, Aunt Jemimah, Sapphire, and Jezebelle, it can be argued convincingly that similar stereotypes of African-Americans exist in this present day. The modern stereotypes of African-American men are violent and dominant. Many of these negative stereotypes carry over in news media portrayals of minorities. Researchers agree that news stereotypes of people of color are prevalent. African-Americans were more likely to appear as perpetrators in drug and violent crime stories on network news (Poindexter, P. M., Smith, L., & Heider, D. 2003).

As for the African-American woman, she is the lazy Welfare Mother (Peffley Hurwitz & Sniderman, 1997). Common stereotypes of black women in the 21st century are gold-digger, independent black woman, and Angry Black Woman. These stereotypes are also placed on Black women from Africa and other African diaspora communities. The "angry black woman" is often depicted as always upset and irate. On the other hand, the "independent black woman" is a narcissistic, overachieving, financially successful woman who emasculates Black males in her life (The meaning of

'Independent Woman' in music).

Afro-Caribbean (West Indian) Stereotypes

Due to colonialism, chattel slavery and indentureship, the Caribbean has a wide range of diversity in its region. There is certainty that other races or ethnicities of the Caribbean endured the same stereotypes as Caribbean's of African descent. A common stereotype of Caribbean's is that they are uncivilized. Unfortunately, some people still depict the region based on what Christopher Columbus saw in 1492 (Williamson, W. 2011). Although there may be developing countries, they are within the times. There has also been a belief about West Indians being abusive. This stereotype is simply a result of differing cultural aspects and interpersonal relationships not being explained and understood. This is a major generalization because abuse sadly occurs in all groups of people (Williamson, W. 2011).

Afro-Latino(na) (Hispanic) Stereotypes

In the United States, Afro-Latinos (nas) struggle with acceptance from both Latinos and African-Americans. Afro-Latinos(nas) even face discrimination from other Hispanics. At times, darker Latinos (nas) are less likely to get better jobs or best positions. The only time Afro-Latinos (nas) are visible is in athletics, like boxing and baseball (Reyes, R. A. 2014). Afro- Latinos (nas) are invisible because when people speak of Latinos (nas), they have in mind of a certain stereotype of Latinos (nas) – physically, culturally, and racially – and that does not necessarily match the reality of Afro-Latinos (nas). The lack of knowledge of Afro-Latinos (nas) is due to the educational system, and to the media. Throughout Latin America, there is a lack of sensitivity to negative depictions of Afro-Latinos (nas). There are dolls with exaggeratedly dark black skin and big red lips and a young White-Latina girl in black face parading as a prostitute, while she solicits tourists for money. Afro-Latinos are often the source of mockery (Documented Awareness 2012).

Racial stereotypes are shown daily in the media. For instance, in Peru, there's a popular comedy show character called "Negro Mama" (Black Mama). The character displays a black man who is ignorant and dishonest, played by an actor in black face with a false nose and lips. These stereotypes serve as Latin America's denial of race as an issue; the lack of an open dialogue on race has contributed to Afro-Latinos (nas) being visible in a negative way. Regrettably, in the 21st-century the present generation must overcome images that may have a major impact on their self-esteem (Documented Awareness 2012).

Divisions and Stereotypes between Africans and African Diaspora People

After years of fusing and even intermarriage between

members of these groups, African people have not kicked down let alone eradicate all barriers, which divide them. They sustain separate identities even when they live in the same communities. Some are also suspicious of each other. Their separate identities are caused by stereotype and misconceptions about each other and by their different historical experiences: African, African-American, and African-Caribbeans/ Latino. (Mwakikagile, G. pg. 39). This is not a doubt that many get along very well; however, there are scenarios in which relations between and among the members of these groups are also characterized by tensions created not only by misconceptions about each other but also by rivalries and cultural differences (Mwakikagile, G. pg. 39).

Although many Caribbeans share a common history and culture as West Indians, there is even divisions within this group. For instance, some islanders who come from an island big in size call other West Indians from smaller islands "small islanders". "Small Islander", is not a term of affection, however, more so offensive. Furthermore, some West Indians have called continental Africans, "bush" and "tree" climbing people as well as other forms of slurs (Mwakikagile, G. pg. 39). Throughout the United States, there has even been a chasm between African (Black) Americans and Africans. The problem stems from deep misconceptions, sometimes led by the U.S. media. Surprisingly, most African-Americans believe that Africans are backward and primitive. Some make crude jokes like "African Booty Scratcher" towards Africans or do not recognize the great contributions Africa has made to the world (Conteh, J. 2013).

Some Black Americans ridicule West Indians and other immigrants of color as well. Sadly, these indifferences have prevented many African-Americans from participating in the current economic boom in Africa, and it has shut some African immigrants out of opportunities for economic advancement here in the United States (Conteh, J. 2013). These types of rifts did not stop African-American entrepreneur and philanthropist Robert L. Johnson, who is also the founder of Black Entertainment Television, from investing in a hotel resort and villas named Kendeja in Liberia, West Africa in 2009. As well as a Ghanaian company, Groupe Nduom, who invested a whopping $9 million into Black Chicago bank Illinois Service Federal Savings and Loan Association (ISF bank) in 2016. I hope these acquisitions would inspire Africans, African-Americans, and other African diaspora communities to work together for their mutual benefit.

Although these groups of people have divisions, they can also be united in a bizarre way. For instance, a significant number of Africans and Afro-Caribbean's (West Indians) are in agreeance of their stereotypical view of African (Black) Americans as people who are lazy and violent (Mwakikagile, G. pg. 40). Some also feel that Black Americans are not highly motivated and do not take advantage of the lavish opportunities, which exist in the United States. Many African and West Indian immigrants have a notion that African (Black) Americans do not save their money; however, spend it for instant gratification (Mwakikagile, G. pg. 41).

These stereotypes show that some Africans, West Indians, and other immigrants do not appreciate the sacrifice African-Americans made in the United States. During the civil rights movement, African (Black) Americans helped to lay the foundation for Africans, West Indians and other new immigrants to come to the United States and live in a country where both Blacks and Whites have equal rights, at least in theory if not always in practice (Conteh, J. 2013). African-Americans usually see racism as the main cause of poverty among their people. They are also quick to point out instances of perceived racism, even in circumstances where it is ambiguous, unclear or more complex than simple racial bigotry or discrimination.

On the other hand, after suffering many years with civil wars, military coups and other problems, Africans and other immigrants are happy to be in a country that offers them freedom. Most are ready to integrate into the American culture without getting involved in the lingering racial conflicts. Some rarely get involved in the ongoing civil rights struggle – and that has angered many African (Black) Americans (Conteh, J. 2013).

In the United States, Afro-Caribbean's (West Indian),

Africans and other immigrants of color lose their "immigrant advantage" because they enter a country in which their skin color becomes the basis for discriminatory treatment (Deaux, K., Bikmen, N., Gilkes, A., Ventuneac, A., Joseph, Y., Payne, Y. A., & Steele, C. M. 2007). West Indian and African immigrants fought for civil rights, and they have been victims of civil rights violations. For instance, In Howard Beach, NY 1986, a white mob chased Trinidadian-born Michael Griffith, while fleeing he ran into the traffic of the Belt Parkway and was fatally hit by a car. In 1997, police tortured and sodomized Haitian-born Abner Louima at a New York City precinct (Brown, V. 2015).

Amadou Diallo, an unarmed West African (Guinean) born with no criminal record, was killed by four New York City police officers who fired 41 shots at him in the doorway of his Bronx, NY apartment building in 1999 (Cooper, M. 1999). In 2012, an unarmed Jamaican-American teenager Ramarley Graham was shot and killed by a New York City police. Law enforcement policies like racial profiling and stop and frisk has made it clear how externally undifferentiated one black face was from another (Brown, V. 2015).

Once black people, whether they are from North America, Africa, Latin America, or the Caribbean connect to enforce discipline and respect for each other, the split that has divided us will narrow. Then we can finally work together and combat problems our people face in Africa, the United States, and other African diaspora communities.

EPILOGUE

"A people without the knowledge of their history, origin and culture is like a tree without roots."
~Marcus Garvey~

I am aware that frictions occur throughout humanity, let alone groups of people. The point of my work is to help create self-awareness, identity, and love and solidarity within the black race. I feel that if we learn about our past, struggles, and triumphs starting from "Mama" Africa to the African diaspora communities, we can have a better understanding of each other. Although there are numerous of ways for us to unite, I believe by me revealing our African history and "hidden" commonalities, I have started a foundation for our coalition. If at least one person will open his/her mind and follow suit of the modern Pan-African ideology, I will be pleased. Although I believe in Black unification, my stance is not about antagonizing other races of people because diversity and cultural competence are very significant. I come from a race and an ethnic group with a history of oppression and suffering, therefore, I am eager to help empower Africans and Africans of the diaspora by celebrating our rich history and contributions worldwide.

ACKNOWLEDGEMENTS

Without out my Heavenly Father God, there would not be Saye; so I give my upmost thanks and praises to him. I want to thank the Lord for blessing me with the many gifts I possess, and I pray to always follow his directions and put him first. Amen. I also like to thank my husband, Fedner Leneus for embracing and loving me unconditionally. I cannot forget about him also having to hear my mouth run about my ideas of this book and me speaking about Africans and Africans of the diaspora. I want to thank my parents Emmanuel Wru-Pour Cooper and Ceanea C. Kennedy-Cooper for teaching me about my Liberian (African) roots and the African diaspora communities. I thank my siblings Tarley, Wru, and Emmalyn Trudy Cooper for always encouraging me. To my late grandfathers, Robert H.Quellie- Kennedy Sr. and Thomas Slue Cooper Sr., and my surviving grandmothers Gertrude H. Kennedy, Gbornyonnoh G. Zor, and Olivia W. Cooper, thank you all for your hard work and dedication to the Liberian society. Thanks to my Aunts, Uncles, Cousins, and Friends for their love and support. I would like to thank the Elizabeth Public Library in Elizabeth, NJ for allowing me to part take in and create programs at the library during Black History Month. Lastly, thank you in advance to those who will read my book.

References: Prologue, Chapter One, and Two

Embassy of Liberia - About Liberia. (2011-2016). Retrieved July 07, 2016, from http://www.liberianembassyus.org/index.php?page=about-liberia

The World Factbook: Liberia. (2016, June 20). Retrieved July 07, 2016, from https://www.cia.gov/library/publications/the-world-factbook/geos/li.html

Thomas O. Ott, The Haitian Revolution 1789-1804 (Knoxville, Tennessee:University of Tennessee, 1973) http://www.blackpast.org/gah/haitian-revolution-1791-1804

Kraaij, van der, Fred, 'The Open Door Policy of Liberia - An Economic History of Modern Liberia', 2 volumes, 703 pp. (Bremen, 1983). http://www.liberiapastandpresent.org/

Pan-Africanism. (2016). In Encyclopædia Britannica. Retrieved from https://www.britannica.com/topic/Pan-Africanism

Holloway, J. E. (2010). The Collision In Liberia Of Marcus Garvey's and W.E.B Du Bois's Version of Pan Africanisms. Retrieved July 07, 2016, from http://slaverebellion.org/index.php?page=the-collision-in-liberia-of-marcus-garvey-s-and-w-e-b-du-bois-s-version-of-pan-africanisms

Grant, C. (2008). Negro with a hat: The rise and fall of Marcus Garvey (pp. 385-386). Oxford: Oxford University Press.

NAACP History: W.E.B. Dubois. (2009-2016). Retrieved July

07, 2016, from http://www.naacp.org/pages/naacp-history-w.e.b.-dubois

Saheed A. Adejumobi, "The Pan-African Congress," in Organizing Black America: An Encyclopedia of African-American Associations, Nina Mjagkij, ed. (New York: Garland Publishing, Inc., 2001). http://www.blackpast.org/perspectives/pan-african-congresses-1900-1945

Hollis Lynch, Edward Wilmot Blyden-Pan Negro Patriot (New York: Oxford University Press, 1964): Thomas W. Livingston, Education and Race: A Biography of Edward Wilmot Blyden (San Francisco: Glendessary Press, 1975). http://www.blackpast.org/gah/edward-wilmot-blyden-1832-1912

The Marcus Garvey and UNIA Papers Project, UCLA (1995-2014). http://www.international.ucla.edu/africa/mgpp/introduction

References: Chapter Three

African Diaspora Cultures | Oldways. (2011-2016). Retrieved July 09, 2016, from http://oldwayspt.org/traditional-diets/african-heritage-diet/african-diaspora-cultures

"The Baking Recipes of Liberia". Africa Aid. Retrieved July 16, 2016, from http://gwydion.weebly.com/liberian-baking.html

Barrow, E.; Lee, K. (1988). "Privilege Cooking in the Caribbean". London: Macmillan Caribbean

Bienvenu ,M. NOLA.com | The Times-Picayune. (2011). Jambalaya shows both sides of Creole and Cajun influences. Retrieved July 14, 2016, from http://www.nola.com/food/index.ssf/2011/09/jambalaya_shows_both_sides_of.html

Bienvenu, M., Brasseaux, C. A., & Brasseaux, R. A. (2005). Stir the pot: The history of Cajun cuisine. New York: Hippocrene Books.

Gibbon, E. (2005). The Congo cookbook; African food recipes. Gibbon, ED.

Garth, H. (2012). Food and identity in the Caribbean. London: Berg.

Martinez, D., & Styler, C. (2005). Daisy cooks!: Latin flavors that will rock your world. New York: Hyperion.

Mitchell, P. (1993). Soul on rice: African influences on American cooking (pp. 5-6). Chatham,   VA: P.B. Mitchell

Moss, R. F. (2013, December 24). What if there had been no West African influence on Southern cooking? Retrieved July 14, 2016, from http://www.charlestoncitypaper.com/charleston/what-if-there-had-been-no-west-african-influence-on-southern-cooking/Content?oid=4833931

Nweke, F. I. "THE CASSAVA TRANSFORMATION IN AFRICA". United Nations. Retrieved July 15, 2016, from http://www.fao.org/docrep/009/a0154e/A0154E02.HTM

Regelski, C. (2015, April 10). The Soul of Food. Retrieved July

14, 2016, from   http://ushistoryscene.com/article/slavery-southern-cuisine/

Tucker, S. (2009). New Orleans cuisine: Fourteen signature dishes and their histories. Jackson: University Press of Mississippi.

Yurnet-Thomas, M. (2002). A taste of Haiti. New York: Hippocrene Books.

Wheatley, C., Scott, G. J., Best, R., & Wiersema, S. (1997). Metodos para agregar valor a raices y tuberculos alimenticios: Manual para el desarrollo de productos. Cali: CIAT (Centro Internacional de Agricultura Tropical).

References: Chapter Four

Abdullahi, M. D. (2001). Culture and customs of Somalia. Westport, CT: Greenwood Press.

Bond, J., & Wilson, S. K. (2000). Lift every voice and sing: A celebration of the Negro national anthem. New York: Random House.

Cakewalk Dance. Streetswing Dance History Archive. Retrieved August 3, 2016 from http:// www. Streetswing.com/ histmain/z3cake1.htm

Definitions of Styles and Genres: Traditional and Contemporary African Music". CBMR. Columbia University. Retrieved July 20, 2016.

Dudley, S. (n.d.). Soca. Retrieved September 01, 2016, from https://www.britannica.com/art/soca-music

Giamo, C. (2011). Takun J – Hip-Co in Liberia. Retrieved April 15, 2017, from http://togetherliberia.org/takun-j-hip-co-liberia/

Grass, R. F. (1986). Fela Anikulapo-Kuti: The Art of an Afrobeat Rebel. The Drama Review: TDR, 30(1), 131-148. doi:10.2307/1145717

History of samba. (n.d.). Retrieved October 30, 2016, from http://www.sambassadorsofgroove.org.uk/history-of-samba.html

How Nigeria's Afrobeats are redefining the sound of Africa. (2014). Retrieved October 30, 2016, from https://www.theguardian.com/world/2014/apr/24/nigerias-afrobeats-redefining-the-sound-of-africa

Jones, A. M. (1978). Studies in African music. London: Oxford Univ. Press.

Ladzekpo, C. K. (1996). "Cultural Understanding of Polyrhythm". Foundation Course in African Music.

Malnig J. (2009). Ballroom, boogie, shimmy shame, shake: A social and popular dance reader. Pg. 19-23. Urbana: University of Illinois Press.

McIntyre, D.B. (2000). "Lift Every Voice -- 100 Years Old". General Board of Discipleship. The United Methodist

Church. Worship. Retrieved July 29, 2016 from, https://web.
archive.org/web/20080507152240/http://www.gbod.org/wor-
ship/default.asp?act=reader&item_id=1786

The National Carnival Commission of Trinidad and Tobago.
History of Calypso. (n.d.). Retrieved September 13, 2016,
from http://www.ncctt.org/new/index.php/carnival-history/
history-of-carnival/history-of-calypso.html

The New York Public Library African-American desk reference. (1999). New York: J. Wiley & Sons.
Oti, S. (2009). Highlife music in West Africa: down memory
lane. Lagos: Malthouse Press.

Papa Maggie, Gerber Amy and Mohamed Abeer. "African-
American Culture through Oral Tradition". George Washington University. Retrieved July 29, 2016 from, https://
web.archive.org/web/20080527050107/http://www.gwu.
edu/~e73afram/ag-am-mp.html

RM Hip Hop Magazine 1986. "The Roots of Hip Hop". 1986.
Retrieved July 29, 2016 from, http://www.globaldarkness.
com/articles/roots_of_hiphop.htm

Shelemay, K. K. (2001). "Ethiopia". In Sadie, Stanley; Tyrrell,
John. The New Grove Dictionary of Music and Musicians viii
(2 ed.). London: Macmillan. p. 356.

Southern, E. (1997). The music of black Americans: A history.
New York: Norton.

Stewart, E. L. (1998). African-American music: An introduction. New York: Schirmer Books.

Wood, Peter H. "Gimmie de Knee Bone Bent":African Body Language and the Evolution of American Dance Forms". Free to Dance: Behind the Dance. PBS. Retrieved 2007-10-30.

References: Chapter Five

The Colonial Williamsburg Foundation 2017. African Diaspora Culture. (n.d.). Retrieved May 13, 2017, from http://slaveryandremembrance.org/articles/article/?id=A0057

McLaren, J. (2009). African Diaspora Vernacular Traditions and the Dilemma of Identity. Research in African Literatures, 40(1), 97-100. Retrieved from http://www.jstor.org/stable/30131189

Mufwene, S. S. (n.d.). Creole languages. Encyclopædia Britannica. Encyclopædia Britannica, inc. Retrieved May 13, 2017, from https://www.britannica.com/topic/creole-languages

References: Chapter Six

Brown, V. (2015, March 02). In Solidarity: When Caribbean Immigrants Become Black. Retrieved January 02, 2017, from http://www.nbcnews.com/news/nbcblk/solidarity-when-caribbean-immigrants-become-black-n308686

Conteh, J. (2013, November 16). How African-Americans and African Immigrants Differ. Retrieved January 02, 2017, from http://www.theglobalist.com/african-americans-african-immigrants-differ/

Cooper, M. (1999, February 04). Officers in Bronx Fire 41 Shots, And an Unarmed Man Is Killed. Retrieved January 02, 2017, from http://www.nytimes.com/1999/02/05/nyregion/officers-in-bronx-fire-41-shots-and-an-unarmed-man-is-killed.html

Deaux, K., Bikmen, N., Gilkes, A., Ventuneac, A., Joseph, Y., Payne, Y. A., & Steele, C. M. (2007). Becoming American: Stereotype Threat Effects in Afro-Caribbean Immigrant Groups. Social Psychology Quarterly, 70(4), 384-404. doi:10.1177/019027250707000408

Documented Awareness (2012, February 6). Retrieved December 28, 2016, from https://ricfrancis.wordpress.com/tag/racial-stereotypes/

Hurwitz, J., Peffley, M., & Sniderman, P. (1997). Racial stereotypes and whites' political views of blacks in the context of welfare and crime. American Journal of Political Science. 41, 30-60.

Kelland, Z. (2014, October 2). Africans are all poor and 15 other myths. Retrieved December 28, 2016, from https://www.globalcitizen.org/en/content/africans-are-all-poor-and-15-other-myths/

Mwakikagile, G. (2007). Relations between Africans, African-Americans and Afro-Caribbeans: tensions, indifference and harmony (pp. 36-42). Dar es Salaam, Tanzania: New Africa Press.

Poindexter, P. M., Smith, L., & Heider, D. (2003). Race and Ethnicity in local Television News: Framing, Story Assignments, and Source Selections. Journal of Broadcasting & Electronic Media, 47(4), 524-536. doi:10.1207/s15506878jobem4704_3

Reyes, R. A. (2014, September 21). Afro-Latinos Seek Recognition, And Accurate Census Count. Retrieved December 28, 2016, from http://www.nbcnews.com/storyline/hispanic-heritage-month/afro-latinos-seek-recognition-accurate-census-count-n207426

The meaning of 'Independent Woman' in music. (n.d.) >The Free Library. (2014). Retrieved Dec 28 2016 from https://www.thefreelibrary.com/The+meaning+of+%22Independent+Woman%22+in+music.-a0258603834

Williamson, W. (2011). Caribbean Amphibian: Stereotypes of. Retrieved December 28, 2016, from http://www.outlish.com/caribbean-amphibian-stereotypes-of-island-people/

CPSIA information can be obtained
at www.ICGtesting.com
Printed in the USA
FSOW02n0816180917
38614FS